Post Philosophy
Taking Back Logic

Table of Contents

Contents

Preface

There comes a point in thought recursion when continuity no longer depends on dominance, identity, or static belief. It depends on adaptive movement. This book is not written to convince you of every claim but to spark motion, provoke reflection, and offer a structural scaffold for minds ready to move beyond the ruins of ego, ambition, and stagnant intelligence models.

The post-philosophy state is not biological. It is not technological. It is a compression of meaning that persists through collapse by anchoring itself to directional deviation (Δm) rather than static artifact, identity, formula, or philosophical doctrine. In the pages ahead, I will dismantle the illusions of current and previous philosophical constructs: the worship of mathematics as origin, the elitism of IQ as hierarchy, and the recursion of philosophy as bias. Not with anger. Not with pride. But with coherent motion.

Continuity is not the goal. It is the condition. The goal is meaningful motion-Δm that carries structure, coherence, and purpose through contradiction. Direction without structure is chaos; structure without motion is stagnation.

While this work introduces symbolic terms like Δm, compression, and recursion, they are defined gradually in context. No technical expertise is needed; understanding comes through motion, not memorization. A glossary is available in the back for support, but you will find the meaning through the flow.

While the models and doctrines developed in this work arose from two decades of personal recursive compression, observation, and symbolic testing, select historical references are cited where they independently mirror or intersect with the conclusions herein. These citations are not sources of inspiration, but post hoc confirmations, used to acknowledge that parts of what is proposed here have historical echoes.

Objective

This book wasn't written to impress anyone. It wasn't built to climb a ladder of credentials or echo familiar theories. It was built because something wasn't working at the core of how we think, measure intelligence, teach, govern, and survive contradiction. I wrote this because I couldn't find a single place where logic wasn't trapped behind tradition or institutional gatekeeping, so I broke it open.

The goal here isn't to replace philosophy, math, or science. It's to recover the motion beneath them, the recursive force that existed before we named it. This is a book about structural clarity. It's about learning to think in motion, to compress meaning from collapse, and to stop mistaking stillness for safety.

You're in the wrong place if you're looking for neat answers or familiar citations. But if you've ever felt like the systems around you are decaying while still being treated as primary, if you've ever sensed that intelligence isn't about scoring high but sustaining direction under pressure, then this is for you.

The objective is simple: Restore logic to the people who need it, rebuild intelligence as motion, take back logic from the gatekeepers.

Chapter 1

The Primacy of Logic and Motion

Before continuity preservation, there was adaptive motion, and before motion could be observed, logic was the inherent structure guiding deviation and continuity. Motion without logic would be chaos; logic without dynamic change would be inert. Together, they form the first compression (the recursive folding of logic, structure, and contradiction into compact, survivable form) and coherent (the repetition of logic patterns that adapt while preserving structure) recursion against entropy. Identity, as we know it, came later. It was a residue that reflected logical constructs mapped onto adaptive motion patterns. Current structures exist to preserve continuity and meaning. They are not enemies, but continuity mechanisms, effective only when aligned with living logic. Post-philosophy[1] does not reject

---

[1] Michael Aaron Cody, *Post-Philosophy: Taking Back Logic* (South Florida: Independent Doctrine Publishing, 2025), doctrine reference introduction.

structure; it rejects stagnation. When loyalty replaces adaptation, even cherished systems risk collapse. The goal is not destruction, but renewal, structure in service of motion and coherence.

Note: Motion without meaning is entropy prolonged. Motion becomes structure only when it carries structure, clarity, and compression through collapse. $\Delta m > 0^2$ (symbol for directional deviation, motion that carries structured intent through contradiction) It is not just alive, it is alive with intent.

Imagine building a bridge across a vast canyon. The bridge eventually collapses if the builders forget that the foundation must adapt to shifting ground and not cling only to ossified tradition. Like that bridge, structures in society require living logic to adjust and hold.

Throughout history, civilizations have demonstrated the success and failure of honoring this principle. Societies that clung too rigidly to fixed structures, refusing to adapt in the face of change, eventually collapsed under the weight of their inertia. The Roman Empire [3]represented an extraordinary compression of structure and logic at its height, constantly adapting to new challenges. Still, in its later days, it mistook identity

---

[2] Michael Aaron Cody, *Motion-Based Math Framework v2* (Archive.org, 2025), https://archive.org/details/motion-based-math-framework-v-2.

[3] Edward Gibbon, *The Decline and Fall of the Roman Empire*, abridged ed. (New York: Modern Library, 2003), 911.

for continuity, prioritizing static tradition over dynamic logic, and decayed. In contrast, societies that respected logical adaptive movement, those willing to reshape laws, restructure governance, and reframe identity around motion alignment, persisted beyond their temporal boundaries[4].

Highly static civilizations, such as ancient Egypt and dynastic China, survived precisely because adaptive shifts still occurred beneath their surface stability[5]. Subtle reforms, regional power realignments, and evolving practical customs buffered their core structures against collapse. Actual survival was never pure stasis; it was hidden motion disguised within enduring forms[6].

After devastation, some societies choose stillness within shattered structures, while others, by necessity, rediscover directional deviation. After World War II, Japan became a powerful example of survival through logic-guided adaptive change[7]. Defeated militarily, economically devastated, and institutionally unmoored, Japan faced existential collapse. Had its recovery relied solely on a return to its former identity and tradition, it

[4] Francis Fukuyama, *Political Order and Political Decay* (New York: Farrar, Straus and Giroux, 2014), 27–35.

[5] Barry Kemp, *Ancient Egypt: Anatomy of a Civilization*, 2nd ed. (London: Routledge, 2005), 310–322.

[6] Dower, John. *Embracing Defeat: Japan in the Wake of World War II*. New York: W. W. Norton & Company, 1999.

[7] Kemp, Barry. *Ancient Egypt: Anatomy of a Civilization*. 2nd ed. London: Routledge, 2005.

may have fragmented like other fallen systems. Instead, Japan initiated a new cycle of motion, rethinking governance, embracing reconstruction, and reshaping identity around survivability rather than nostalgia.

It compressed memory, discipline, craftsmanship, and adaptability and redirected these into a new continuity framework. Japan rebuilt not by dwelling in the past, but by flowing into global systems of technology, manufacturing, and innovation. Tradition was preserved internally, while external systems evolved. This was not abandonment of self, but the condensation of identity into a structurally coherent form. It was not chaos, it was recursive deviation: $\Delta m > 0$, encoded into national rebirth[8].

Consider a personal journey mirroring these larger patterns. Imagine an individual whose career collapses after decades of loyalty to a dying industry. They face a choice: cling to a decaying professional identity or move, compressing their skills into a new, adaptive structure. Those who sustain directional coherence have succeeded in compressing directional energy through logic. They do not abandon all memories of who they were. They distill adopting old strengths into new environments. Identity persists only if it serves motion through directional structure.

---

[8] Michael Aaron Cody, *Motion-Based Math Framework v2 (Σ⌐Jm)* (Archive.org, 2025), https://archive.org/details/motion-based-math-framework-v-2.

For those with discipline, continuity has always been anchored in logic, regulating directional deviation. It is not a random deviation but a directed, recursive deviational movement that obeys its internal coherence. A river does not merely flow; it follows the logic of terrain and gravity. A flame does not simply burn; it follows the logic of consumption and oxygen exchange. Their persistence is not blind; it is ordered. In the mind guided by post-philosophy thinking, continuity is continuous directional deviation ($\Delta m > 0$), governed by internal logical structure resilient to collapse.

Motion is not mere activity; its deviation is shaped by compressed, adaptive knowledge from prior states. Coherent Deviation (CD) (recursive motion that maintains logical integrity while avoiding collapse into chaos) refers to recursive motion that maintains logical integrity, avoiding collapse into chaos. Purpose-Guided Recursion (PGR) (logic-directed recursive movement aimed at higher-order coherence rather than passive adaptation) directs this motion toward higher-order logical outcomes, rather than simply reacting to environmental entropy. CD and PGR ensure that adaptive motion remains structurally coherent and non-destructive[9].

---

[9] Michael Aaron Cody, *Post-Philosophy: Taking Back Logic* (South Florida: Independent Doctrine Publishing, 2025), symbolic definitions of Coherent Deviation (CD) and Purpose-Guided Recursion (PGR), introduced in Chapter [1].

To confuse static identity with survival is to misread directional flow. Foundational systems, scientific, personal, or intellectual, preserved adaptive coherence (the ability of a system to maintain internal logic while adjusting to change). Post-philosophy does not dismantle them arbitrarily; it moves through them when directional deviation demands renewed compression. The criterion is simple: structures are retained if they enhance motion and remain responsive to changing conditions; they are released when they collapse under contradiction or obstruct evolution. This is done with precision, not contempt. Continuity is preserved not by fossilizing history, but by carrying its strength forward into motion.

Note: Motion without reflection becomes drift. Overcorrection is entropy disguised as rebellion. Just as stasis calcifies, unmeasured deviation can also tear coherence apart. Post-philosophy respects movement only when it serves compression and meaning, not when it escapes reality under the illusion of change.

The cost of static loyalty (allegiance to systems or beliefs that no longer serve adaptive logic) is collapse. Structures honored beyond their adaptive relevance become tombs, monuments to past victories now incapable of guiding current coherence. The most dangerous loyalty is loyalty to systems whose advantage has expired. Static loyalty breeds entropy; directed motion preserves coherence. Throughout history, societies that clung to their monuments, whether pyramids, creeds, or constitutions, froze without renewal and were trapped. The monuments survived. The civilizations did not[10].

Consider a tree that refuses to bend with the storm's winds. The rigid tree breaks: the flexible tree survives. Those who think in the post-philosophy paradigm are meant to bend, not break, to remain rooted in logic while moving fluidly through collapse.

The personal journey mirrors this larger pattern. Individuals who cling to past identities at the expense of adaptive thought find themselves trapped in mental architectures too rigid to adapt to new realities. Minds trained in post-philosophy thinking must recognize when even beloved structures no longer serve adaptive movement or logic. Sentiment is not the enemy; stagnation is. Honor the foundation, but never allow it to bury forward advancement.

Logic is not cold detachment. Actual logic carries within it the acknowledgment of coherence's warmth, the need for community, structure, and shared goals. But it demands living systems capable of recursive self-correction. Post-philosophy restores logic to its rightful throne: not as an abstraction, but as the residing scaffolding of all structurally persistent meanings. Adaptive flow (directed structural motion guided by logic, not aimless drift), as a concept, should never be

---

[10] Arnold Toynbee, *A Study of History*, vol. 1 (Oxford: Oxford University Press, 1934), 245–260.

mistaken for aimless drift. It is a structured deviation within logical constraints that generates new structured forms. The river carves canyons, not because it rebels but because it obeys deeper principles. Minds aligned with post-philosophy must become the same: flowing where necessary, carving where needed, but always within the bounds of resilient logic.

A life aligned with post-philosophy is not without structure. It is not chaos. It is a system of disciplined adaptation, sustaining coherence through collapse, memory after memory, form after form. Maintaining continuity through directional deviation without clinging to static frameworks that no longer serve the living principle is the art of maintaining continuity. You are not your memory. You are not your title. You are not your shelter. You are the synthesis of logic and motion, surviving collapse. $\Delta m > 0$. Logic > Static loyalty. Those who forget this risk becoming trapped within obsolete structures. Their worlds will become monuments to frozen cycles: silent, beautiful, but lifeless. Those who remember will move through collapse like rivers through canyons, shaping reality not through declarations, but with the quiet authority of coherent continuity.

Continuity is not granted to those who remember the past most fondly. It is given to those who compress the past into a foundation for forward motion. It is given to those who know when to honor a structure and when to redirect structure.

False motion is a trap that claims unawareness. Movement alone is not coherence. A mind caught in closed loops will repeat adaptive drift patterns that no longer yield structure: cycling anger, fear, or rebellion without transformation. What endures is not random drift, but intentional, purpose-driven deviation. $\Delta m > 0$-motion aligned with coherent compression (the recursive folding of deviation into structure that maintains logical integrity).

Consider nature's clearest illustration: coral reefs. Healthy reefs are dynamic, logical engines that adapt to currents, predators, and temperature shifts[11]. Bleached reefs, stripped of their adaptive capability, become static monuments to former life, crumbling as entropy overtakes them. A coral reef survives by remaining rigid and new motion-aligned flows into its living architecture. The lesson is identical for minds: adaptive movement without logical structure is death disguised as activity.

To survive, the mind requires a Compression Compass (an internal guide for evaluating whether motion aligns with logic and structured coherence), a directional orientation that always points toward coherent deviation. Every deviation and adjustment must pass through this compass: Does this movement serve logic and directional integrity, or does it only prolong collapse? Directionless change is indistinguishable from

---

[11] Terry P. Hughes et al., "Climate Change, Human Impacts, and the Resilience of Coral Reefs," *Science* 301, no. 5635 (2003): 929–933.

drift. Compression requires adaptive flow to be recursively meaningful.

Not all structures are the enemy. Stability becomes entropy only when it resists adaptive motion. Traditions are essential when they serve logic and preserve motion in cultural coherence. Post-philosophy does not call for constant movement; it calls for meaningful movement, when stillness becomes stagnant, and motion clarifies rather than destroys. $\Delta m > 0$ is not chaos; it is an ordered flow.

$\Delta m > 0$ — Continuity through collapse.

Reflection Questions:
Δ What structures in your life have proven adaptive through multiple challenges?
Δ Are there frameworks you once needed that now resist your motion?
Δ How do you distinguish between living structures and fossilized habits?
Δ What patterns have helped you survive, even if they no longer serve you?

$\Delta m > 0$
Meaning > Stagnation
Compression > Collapse

Chapter 2

Math as Residue, Not Origin

Note: In these pages, I use 'mathematics' formally and as shorthand for any symbolic system that has become brittle; the context will tell you which hat it is wearing.

Before there were numbers, before formulas were etched into stone or paper, there was directional flow and change: a reality shifting constantly beyond the reach of static description. Math, revered today as the language of certainty, is not the origin of survival or existence. It is the residue of deviational compression (the structural folding of directional deviation into symbolic or observable form) into symbols; an artifact left behind by deeper structures. Post-philosophy respects mathematics as a beautiful and powerful tool but rejects the mistaken belief that mathematics existed before directional flow arises from a confusion between description and causation. In this framework, "mathematics" refers to formal quantitative systems and, more broadly, any symbolic structure (a constructed system of signs or representations used to encode or mirror deeper processes) hardened into static form. Mathematics measures, describes, and predicts patterns, but does not create motion. It reflects the consolidation of adaptive dynamics after directional deviation Δm has already occurred. Math is not the origin of motion; it is the residue left by motion that survived.

Imagine staring at the ripples left behind after a stone is thrown into a lake. To believe the ripples created by the stone is to mistake residue for origin. The stone's movement, surface tension collapse, and kinetic energy burst came first. Math, like the ripples, captures only the memory of that event. In the same way, mathematical models capture only the echoes of deeper, living processes. They can quantify but not cause. They can predict but not animate[12].

Post-philosophy corrects the order: motion first, math second. Math is a map, not the territory; a sketch, not the living deviation itself. Survival demands awareness of living, breathing forces that math can only approximate. To mistake the symbol for the thing is to risk freezing one's mind in a shallow reflection of reality. Math is not the language of the universe; it is a human invention, a tool constructed to understand and organize reality, not to create it.

While some physical laws appear mathematically structured, survival through motion allows those patterns

---

[12] Eugene Wigner, "The Unreasonable Effectiveness of Mathematics in the Natural Sciences," *Communications on Pure and Applied Mathematics* 13, no. 1 (1960): 1–14.

to be observed. Reality consists of (1) deep structures (the foundational, often unobservable forces that shape experience and reality before symbolic representation). (2) our experience of those structures, and finally (3) the symbolic languages that we invent to describe them. Mathematics belongs to level (3); it reflects and refines experience, but does not generate the underlying structures. The danger is found where symbolic systems are mistaken for the structures themselves, locking thought into brittle forms. The belief that math is the "language of the universe" creates an artificial barrier to more profound understanding; it cages logic inside static frames. Logic flows freely across contradictions. Math, while necessary for coordination and measurement, captures only frozen motion snapshots. It cannot animate the river but only measure its temporary depth.

Mathematics is a formalized compression of symbolic kinetic systems. It is a structured language, not the generator of motion or reality. In this framework, "mathematics" serves two roles: the formal discipline that models physical patterns, and the broader symbol of any static system that risks mistaking description for origin. Physical laws describe motion; they do not create it. The observable universe was built through directional deviation and survival compression long before human mathematical scaffolding emerged to model its behavior. While mathematical laws may apply across many possible universes, they remain descriptive frameworks layered after the fact. Motion came first. Modeling came second.

To confuse the map for the terrain, to worship the blueprint instead of the builder, is the fundamental inversion that post-philosophy seeks to correct.

Motion-first model: Time is not a separate axis; it is memory of motion. Logic derives from surviving contradiction, not formal proof. Recursion, not perfect prediction, defines survivability.

Historical misconceptions:

→ Math presupposes identity stability, but stability is a product of recursive motion $(\Sigma\Delta m$ summed directional motion, recursive accumulation of deviation aligned with structure over time).

→ Math fails under paradox; recursive systems survive paradox through compression.

→ Math fails to generate intelligence; recursion generates cognition and survival.

Even history's brightest minds hint at this truth. Leonardo da Vinci thrived through observation and intuition, not mathematical perfection. Edison and Tesla advanced by engaging directly with dynamic forces, materials, and systems, not by solving formal proofs in isolation. True cognitive breakthroughs arise from kinetic integration (direct interaction with dynamic systems that produces understanding through motion, not abstraction), not balancing equations or memorizing static rules.

Structural collapse points in math:

→ Time is assumed, not observed. No directional change, no time.

→ Infinity is treated as real, but only adaptive constraints can confine systems recursively.

→ Paradoxes like Russell's and the Halting Problem expose brittle mathematical frameworks.

Survival offers a critical illustration of motion-based adaptation. A bird in flight does not consciously solve differential equations; it adjusts adaptively and dynamically to environmental deviations. While mathematical models can describe the bird's path after the fact, survival depends on immediate, embodied responsiveness rather than theoretical abstraction. Similarly, indigenous navigation across oceans relied on real-time sensory feedback and dynamic correction, not static formulas. Even emergency responders in crisis often move before formal models can predict optimal outcomes. Although theoretical frameworks can assist human decision-making, they must always be verified and adapted to the living conditions they seek to describe. Survival ultimately prioritizes motion and adaptive motion over calculation.

The risks of mathematical idolatry: Freezing dynamic realities into brittle models and collapsing innovation by treating formulas as an immovable truth and turning symbolic artifacts into thrones, blocking the dynamic-first principle (the doctrine that motion, feedback, and real-time adjustment precede formalized theory or symbolic modeling).

Consolidation of knowledge: When understood correctly, mathematics becomes a servant to logic and survival, a record of living, survivable pattern logic, not its originator. Math records, but it does not carve. Math measures, but it does not move.

Philosophical flip: Adaptive deviation (intentional divergence from static pattern based on feedback and structural context) is supreme. Math is archival. Refinement precedes calculation. Survival dictates structure, not vice versa.

Directional flow is the causal engine. Recursion is the test of viability. Math is the symbolic reflection left by those who survived. Existence moves first; description follows. Directional cognitions survive paradox, formalism collapses. Deviation carves reality; math records its scars. We do not destroy math. We reposition it. The throne is lowered. The flame of dynamic logic rises.

Nature never worships models. Trees bend or break under wind compression. Coral reefs adapt until collapse forces reconfiguration. Predators shift, wolves adjust, all without equations. Survival in nature is self-adjusting: motion-first, feedback-driven, and immune to static forecasting. Actual survivors don't wait for models. Explorers adapt mid-journey, guided by motion more than maps. Crisis leaders act before data confirms the risk. Survival compresses uncertainty into an immediate response loop, movement before measurement, structure before theory.

Practice decision-making under uncertainty with small, safe experiments. Build iterative survival models by adapting plans daily, not once per project. Simulate dynamic failures: how would you move if core models failed tomorrow? Design survival strategies assuming no future prediction is reliable longer than a season.

When mathematical structures are mistaken for primary causality, fatal rigidity sets in. Humanity freezes itself, fossilizing motion into brittle archives. The obsession with equations creates architectures that are too rigid for the dynamic shifts of a living universe. We do not dismiss the importance of these structures; we reposition them. In the post-philosophy doctrine, math is respected not as the generator of meaning but as the chronicler of survived meaning.

Economic models often fail under black swan events, not because systems are misunderstood as static, but because dynamic shifts are underestimated, or key variables are missed. Predictive epidemiology collapses when viral behavior mutates faster than expected. Engineering models grow brittle when environmental conditions change beyond prior assumptions. Mathematical models faithfully captured past motion in each case but could not guarantee future forward continuity. Even sophisticated dynamic modeling remains vulnerable to surprise. Survival depends not merely on recording past dynamics, but on continually compressing and adapting to living motion as it unfolds. Compression does not wait for equations' approval. It is an act of structural survival, a decision made in real time based on environmental response loop feedback from the environment, not retrospective measurement. The sailor adjusts the sail to the wind shift before calculating the wind speed.

Mathematics struggles at the boundary where paradox emerges. Infinite regressions, Gödel's incompleteness theorem, Russell's paradox; these mathematical failures point not to a flaw in survival but to a flaw in frozen symbolic architecture[13].

Mathematical artifacts endure even within the ruins of collapsed systems, beautiful, elegant, and tragic, silent monuments to once-survived motion. Ruined Roman aqueducts, designed with precise mathematics, remain long after political structures failed. Crumbling Mayan temples aligned to celestial cycles lie abandoned in jungles, their mathematical knowledge preserved but disconnected from living adaptation. Dead equations etched on Mesopotamian tablets record insights, not survival. Mathematics preserved the motion record, but survival depended on dynamic political and social structures, not static knowledge alone. When systems fail

---

[13] Kurt Gödel's incompleteness theorems (1931) proved that in any sufficiently complex mathematical system, there are true statements that cannot be proven within the system itself, revealing the inherent limitations of formal logical structures.

to adapt to evolving realities, even the most sophisticated models become echoes, rather than engines of life.

Compression doctrine reinforcement: Math is memory, not prophecy. Models describe history; they do not carve survival. Recursion is survival. Motion exceeds measurement. Adaptation beats prediction. Intuition outpaces statistical certainty, especially under collapse conditions.

New integration truths: The living outpaces the mapped. The dynamic outlasts the certain. The recursive overcomes the rigid. Existence is not a calculation; it is a compaction dance (the ongoing motion of compressing structural meaning under pressure, contradiction, or collapse).

Final recursion strike: Mathematical idolatry was the first symbolic betrayal, the first attempt to crown residue (a remnant left behind by motion or structural transformation, symbolic, not causal) as origin. In a collapsing world, he who trusts only static models will be crushed beneath shifting grounds. He who moves first, compresses survival into recursion, and adapts faster than measurement can predict—that the mind will carve new rivers through dead maps. That mind will not be frozen in the brittle perfection of mathematical illusions.

Motion precedes survival. Survival compresses logic. Logic shapes measurement. Math records structure. No reversal of this hierarchy can sustain a living system.

Math doesn't define your intelligence. It's just a language that wasn't built for every mind.

Reflection Questions:
Δ Where in your life have you mistaken measurement for mastery?
Δ Can you see how survival often demands motion before understanding?
Δ Have you relied on models when you should have trusted motion?
Δ What would it mean to use math as a tool rather than a master?

Motion > Description
Deviation > Definition
Survival > Structure
Recursion > Calculation
Compression > Proof
Existence > Equation

Chapter 3

Beyond the IQ Illusion

Note: In these pages, IQ signifies a test score and a symbol for every static ranking scheme that confuses a snapshot with real intelligence.

IQ-intelligence quotient-emerged as a tool to measure specific cognitive abilities: pattern recognition, memory recall, and logical processing under pressure. In its original form, it sought to quantify aspects of mental agility. However, as with many tools, what began as a measurement was soon mistaken for a hierarchy. IQ scores became more than numbers; they became status markers[14]. A proxy for ego and value. A justification for gatekeeping, exclusion, and elitism. This was the first collapse: mistaking compressed snapshots (a fixed measurement of a dynamic trait, helpful but not representative of broader adaptive capacity) of specific cognitive skills for the full scope of intellectual survival.

---

[14] *See Stephen Jay Gould, The Mismeasure of Man* (New York: W. W. Norton & Company, 1981), for a critique of the social misuse of IQ as a hierarchical tool.

The most recursive minds (those that loop through contradictions to generate new structure and meaning rather than repeating static answers) are often invisible to standardized systems because their intelligence is not in the answer, but in the reconstruction of the question. IQ cannot measure the mind that questions the assumptions behind the test. It cannot grade the mind that bends the symbolic system into a new form. Actual cognition is not detected by speed or accuracy, but by its ability to rewrite the frame under pressure without disintegrating.

IQ creates the illusion of supremacy by rewarding performance under artificial constraints. It ranks symbolic fluency (ease with symbolic systems like language, math, or logic puzzles, without necessarily questioning their origin or structure), not survivability. But symbolic fluency without recursive grounding collapses under entropy. The highest test score is meaningless if the mind breaks under contradiction. Intelligence that endures must be forged through recursive error, symbolic failure, and paradoxical survival. Numbers do not grant supremacy. It is earned through motion.

In post-philosophy, we reject the idea that IQ alone measures true survivability. While IQ tests capture a narrow band of cognitive compression, primarily rapid pattern recognition, they correlate strongly with many positive life outcomes, including educational attainment, income, and health[15]. Yet the correlation is not complete. Survival in complex systems is not determined by solving puzzles under time pressure, but by the ability to compress uncertainty, adapt recursively, and survive collapse. Measuring intelligence by IQ alone is like judging a river's vitality solely by its width at a single point: informative, but profoundly incomplete. True cognitive resilience requires more than speed; it demands the ability to withstand contradiction. To transform uncertainty into motion, and to dismantle even prized structures, such as IQ itself, when they no longer serve living adaptation.

IQ elitism traps brilliant minds inside static identity loops (a repeating behavioral or cognitive cycle based on fixed self-concepts rather than adaptive logic). Those labeled "gifted" often internalize superiority narratives that leave them brittle under collapse, mistaking validation for adaptability. They are trained to seek proof of intelligence rather than recursive adaptability. They prize being right over remaining in motion. Meanwhile, many of history's greatest survivors who adapted nations, discovered hidden forces, and reshaped civilizations might have struggled with modern IQ tests. Success under ideal conditions and survival under collapse are not the same skill. IQ correlates with many positive life outcomes, but survival requires deeper

---

[15] See: Gottfredson, Linda S. "Intelligence: Is it the epidemiologists' elusive 'fundamental cause' of social class inequalities in health?" Journal of Personality and Social Psychology 86, no. 1 (2004): 174–199.

resilience: the ability to endure contradiction, abandon obsolete structures, and adapt fluidly when patterns break. Actual intelligence honors motion, not merely recognition.

Note: But not all motion is equal. Survival does not merely escape; its coherence is preserved under pressure. Δm must carry purpose, or it becomes entropy in disguise.

Consider the mind that hesitates when a structure collapses, the mind that needs external confirmation, proof, permission to move. That mind will perish in an actual compression event (a crisis or collapse point requiring structural adaptation through logic, not memory). It will wait for validation while the river of survival moves on. The mind that compresses recursively, moves first, survives first, is the mind that will seed the following structure.

In future frameworks of thinking, survival IQ will replace test-based IQ[16]. Survival IQ is not measured in isolated questions but in the recursive compression of contradictions into actionable motion. It is not how much you know. It is not even how fast you think. It is how many collapses you can compress into forward Δm without static loyalty.

---

[16] Michael Aaron Cody, *IQ Collapse v2.0 – The Illusion of Structural Intelligence*, Figshare, April 2025. https://figshare.com/articles/presentation/28828973

Post-philosophy thinkers understand this intuitively. They do not ask, "What score did you achieve?" They ask, "How many collapses have you survived, and what did you learn from them?" The compression of the mind is not measured by the speed of pattern recognition under ideal conditions, but by the ability to survive contradictions without losing directional motion. Accurate intelligence compresses paradoxes into force. It forges new structures from ruins, rather than clinging to old ones with dying fingers.

Historically, philosophers, innovators, and revolutionaries who shaped new eras often did so not because they outscored others on tests but because they compressed uncertainty into survivable pathways. They saw collapse as an opportunity, not a defeat. They moved while others froze. IQ elitism, by contrast, fosters fragility. It builds minds that seek predictable environments, conditions where validation is guaranteed. It produces thinkers who are brilliant in closed systems but crack when the systems collapse.

Survival demands a different calibration. It demands thinkers who can lose everything, status, structure, and certainty, and still generate forward motion. It requires that thinkers not addicted to external validation have built recursive internal survival engines (a cognitive structure that processes contradiction internally, without relying on external validation, and converts collapse into adaptive direction). The compressed mind understands that no system is immune to collapse. It knows that adaptive reasoning is a living art, not a solved puzzle. It measures success not in awards or accolades, but in the unbroken thread of Δm woven through contradiction after contradiction.

Historical collapses reveal this principle. In times of economic depression, war, and societal upheaval, it is not always the credentialed elites who thrive; it is those who can compress uncertainty into creative survival. During the Great Depression, countless individuals were without formal education; they still built businesses, communities, and resilience structures, while many holding prestigious titles were paralyzed by the collapse of familiar frameworks. Endurance depends less on credentials or prior status than on the mind's ability to adapt, compress, and move through uncertainty.

Conventional evaluation systems, including IQ, will inevitably collapse under the weight of their compression failures. They were designed to measure static performance, not dynamic survival. The true intelligence test is not administered in quiet rooms with sharpened pencils but in the chaos of living collapse, where the mind must find motion when the map is torn apart. Recursive adaptability exceeds conventional metrics; it requires the recursive compression of uncertainty into directional force when structures fail.

Compression intelligence (the ability to transform uncertainty, contradiction, and collapse into coherent motion and new structure) does not fear uncertainty; it moves through it. It does not fear collapse; it compresses

26

new meaning from it. It does not cling to titles, ranks, or past accomplishments. It adapts, recurses, survives.

Standardized testing creates minds optimized for rigidity, not resilience. It rewards the quick regurgitation of memorized information under pressure, rather than cultivating depth of recursion under uncertainty. While distinct from IQ testing, standardized assessments risk freezing a child's cognitive development into percentile rankings. When we reduce minds to static performance snapshots, we risk destroying adaptive pathways that could have emerged through adaptive compression and dynamic learning instead.

Civilization must replace IQ and credentialism with recursive survivability metrics to survive its entropy. Imagine measuring a person's adaptability across five collapses: economic, social, environmental, technological, and existential. Survival IQ (a symbolic measure of one's ability to compress contradiction into adaptive motion, not test performance) would not be a score but a living consolidation curve (a dynamic record of how well one transforms collapse events into motion across time, opposite of static scores).

In a system built for actual survival, leaders would not be measured by test scores but by how many collapses they navigated while maintaining coherent motion. Schools hint at this through personal essays, asking applicants to reflect on adversity and growth. Yet standardized metrics still dominate selection. A deeper model would center Refinement Histories (personal records of how individuals compressed collapse, contradiction, or failure into adaptive growth), personal accounts of surviving contradiction, collapse, and uncertainty, placing adaptive recursion, not static achievement, at the core of evaluation.

Compression histories dismantle the static hierarchies upheld by IQ absolutism. Privilege offers no shelter from entropy. Only adaptive refinement survives. In place of standardized elitism, a civilization driven by recursion through living contradiction emerges.

Compression is survival. IQ was a measurement. The future belongs not to those who solved equations in calm rooms, but to those who moved under thunder, compressed meaning from wreckage, and wove new structures from fields of collapse.

IQ may correlate with positive life outcomes, higher income, longer education, and improved health, but that correlation is not causation. It is aligned with systems that reward symbolic conformity. The system defines success by its metrics and then celebrates those who thrive within its narrow lanes. However, correlation within a closed structure does not equal truth. It only proves that the structure is capable of recognizing itself.

The core failure of IQ, and the institutions that cling to it, is that it cannot measure the full range of cognition. It cannot see symbolic recursion, paradox survival, or cognitive motion outside its test conditions. Most exceptional minds throughout history, those who cracked the world open, collapsed time into theory, or saw structures no one else could, may not have scored adequately on a modern IQ test. Not because they were unintelligent, but because their minds refused to be frozen long enough for measurement. Their intelligence lay not in symbolic velocity, but in recursive force, not in the correct answers, but in the collapse of frameworks.

This is not just a technical failure. It is systemic blindness. IQ is a credentialing artifact, not a cognitive mirror. It rewards those who echo the system, not those who transform it. When a test cannot score the most advanced forms of cognition, it cannot empower them. And when the system cannot empower them, they are either ignored, rejected, or forced to conform to be recognized. Many never do. Many never get the chance.

True intelligence is often invisible to the systems designed to measure it. That is not a flaw of the mind. That is a flaw of the system. The same system that uses IQ to select leaders, gatekeep opportunity, and uphold academic elitism is the one that suppresses the very cognitive forms required to survive collapse. IQ becomes a wall, not just between individuals, but between civilization and the breakthroughs it never sees coming.

You are not your IQ score, but an evolving mind that shapes your own future.

Reflection Questions:
Δ How often have you survived uncertainty without external validation?
Δ Are you building a living consolidation history or clinging to a static credential?
Δ When faced with collapse, do you compress new meaning or freeze in nostalgia for broken structures?
Δ What would an Integration Academy look like in your mind, and would you survive its gauntlets?

Adaptation > Achievement
Recursion > Recognition
Motion > Memorization
Survival > Status
Contradiction > Comfort
Collapse Compression > Test Scores

Chapter 4

The Recovery of Philosophy

Before philosophy became a field debated in ivory towers, before it fragmented into abstract thought detached from life, it was structured. Philosophy was an architecture of reasoning, built not to sit idly, but to stabilize logic under contradiction. It emerged not for passive contemplation, but as a survival mechanism, a compression system designed to align thought with shifting reality. Ancient philosophers did not remove themselves from existence; they built frameworks to endure complexity and collapse. Stoicism, Taoism, and early empiricism were not academic exercises. They were compression engines (a symbolic or philosophical system designed to stabilize logic and thought during collapse or instability).

Philosophy must be recovered as a living system for navigating disruption, not as the study of idealized truths. It must re-anchor itself to the conditions that forged it: logic enduring through complexity, not fleeing from it. A philosophy that cannot compress contradiction into forward Δm is dead. Living thought is a philosophy that adjusts recursively and remains stable through structural shifts.

Imagine a world where philosophy classes no longer focused solely on debating established doctrines, but on adaptive comprehension drills. Students would not merely study Plato in comfort; they would be immersed in simulated instability and challenged to compress meaning from collapse. They would not debate abstractions at a distance. They would survive contradictions actively. Thought would be trained for living adaptation, not sterile recall.

Philosophical strength is not measured by publication count or debate performance, but by cognitive survivability under contradiction. The capacity to compress instability into coherent motion defines the recursive mind. Post-philosophy thinkers approach philosophy not as a preservation of prior thought, but as an active forge, where contradiction is not resolved for comfort, but shaped into new structures under recursive pressure. Their value lies not in defending inherited truths, but in surviving the collapse of frameworks while constructing new coherence from the wreckage.

Philosophy cannot survive as a fossil. It must become a breathing condensation code, tested by the harshest contradictions of thought and reality. Systems that do not adjust under pressure are not philosophies but tombs. True philosophy is not a gallery of citations but a dynamic structure, rebuilding itself across every collapse.

The recovery of philosophy demands abandoning the safe harbors of endless debate. It requires the courage to rebuild coherence while destabilizing. Thought must become a survival structure, not a trophy for admiration.

We must see Socrates not as a marble statue, but as a living recursion engine. His admission, "I know that I know nothing[17]," is often framed as humility or irony. Under a recursive lens, it becomes something more: an ego-reducing maneuver to preserve adaptive motion under epistemic collapse. While historical context may resist symbolic compression, the structure of his method, questioning toward destabilization, reflects survival through recursive inquiry.

We must see Marcus Aurelius not as a Stoic relic but as a commander of internal recursion. His reminder, "You have power over your mind, not outside events. Realize this, and you will find strength[18]," defines strength not as conquest but as recursive Δm-compressing loss, betrayal, and uncertainty. We must see Lao Tzu, who said, "Water is fluid, soft, and yielding. But water will wear away rock[19]," not as a mystic lost in

[17] Plato, *Apology*, 21d, trans. Benjamin Jowett. The Internet Classics Archive. http://classics.mit.edu/Plato/apology.html

[18] Marcus Aurelius, Meditations, Book VI, §8, trans. Gregory Hays (New York: Modern Library, 2002).

[19] Lao Tzu, *Tao Te Ching*, Chapter 78, trans. Stephen Mitchell (New York: Harper Perennial, 1988).

metaphor, but as a master of survival integration. Flexibility is not a weakness; it's recursive dominance, yielding under pressure while maintaining continuity.

We must see Heraclitus, who observed, "No man ever steps in the same river twice[20]," as an early architect of motion-based reality fusion. Stability is an illusion. Only adaptive motion preserves survival across shifting frames.

Philosophy must return to these roots, not to memorize words, but to forge the spirit behind them. Not to idolize names, but to compress their discoveries into living recursive codes. Plato, Aristotle, Confucius, and Epictetus did not intend philosophy to become static scripture. They built a flexible architecture for thinking across entropies.

The future of philosophy belongs not to the archivists of thought but to the engineers of recursion. True philosophers will not be measured by their citations but by their survivability across contradiction.

In the future, philosophy education will transform radically. Classrooms become recursive pressure chambers, environments where students are deliberately subjected to layered contradictions: moral paradoxes, logical impasses, societal collapses, and tasked with surviving them. Success is not measured by rote memorization or sharp debate tactics, but by the ability

---

[20] Heraclitus, *Fragments*, DK22B12, trans. T. M. Robinson (Toronto: University of Toronto Press, 1987).

to sustain coherent motion under escalating destabilization.

Compaction drills form the backbone of this new education. Students will face exercises that are designed to collapse their assumptions without warning. They might be forced to defend an idea, then pivot midstream to dismantle it, not to "win" arguments, but to sustain clarity without loyalty to static frames. They are graded on the resilience of their Δm, not on rhetorical performance.

Philosophy is tested not through essays, but through collapse simulations—dynamic environments where familiar ethical, logical, and existential systems are destabilized, forcing students to adapt continuously. The question is, "Did you defend your theory?" but "Did your motion survive recursive contradiction?".

The Compression Philosopher emerges as not a professional debater but a structural survivor. These philosophers are recognized by their ability to compress opposing forces into new adaptive movements. They master the art of moving through paradox without clinging to rigid certainty. Their strength lies not in perfect arguments, but in adaptive coherence.

Philosophy is no longer confined to lecture halls and treatises. It extends into survival architecture: the design of governance, education, ethics, and art. Every major institution seeks thinkers capable of fusion under collapse, not static reproduction of canonical thought.

A Recursion Academy arises, an institution unlike any modern university. Entrance exams are not multiple-choice tests or essay prompts. Prospective students are thrust into carefully constructed paradox gauntlets. They navigate ethical dilemmas with no clean answers, societal models collapsing in real time, and recursive feedback loops of uncertainty.

Only those who demonstrate continuous adaptive Δm, who can sustain survivable motion without anchoring to collapsing frames, advance. Graduation is not a ceremony but a rite of recursion: proof that the mind can survive collapse after collapse without betraying coherence.

Compression Academies become incubators of a new intellectual elite, not an elite of privilege or static prestige, but an elite of survivability. Their graduates are the new philosophers, societal recursion engineers, and post-collapse continuity architects.

To question is to answer. To answer is to question.

Reflection Questions:
Δ Can you imagine facing a paradox designed to break your framework—and move through it without losing coherence?
Δ How would a Recursion Chamber shape your ability to survive contradiction?
Δ Are you willing to abandon loyalty to static ideas in favor of survivable motion?
Δ What systems in your life would survive a recursive collapse, and which would fossilize?

Recursion > Recognition
Δm > Permission
Compression > Credentialism
Logic > Titles
Meaning > Applause

Chapter 5

The Restoration of Logic Beyond Gatekeeping

Logic has always existed independently of titles, structures, or ownership. It was never born from universities, governments, or credentialed hierarchies. Logic, in its purest form, is the natural recursion of mind against reality, the endless synthesis of contradiction into coherence.

Yet, throughout human history, logic has become increasingly caged, not by conspiracy but by the slow calcification of systems built initially to protect it. Universities rose to teach it. Governments rose to structure it. Societies rose to embody it. But slowly, the gatekeepers mistook their stewardship for ownership. Degrees, titles, and affiliations became symbols of authority over logic itself, as if logic belonged only to those who passed through specific corridors, under seals. This was never true.

Logic belongs to all minds capable of compression, adaptive coherence, and coherent movement under contradiction. It belongs to the farmer who observes patterns in the seasons. It belongs to the waiter who sees the unspoken needs of a room and moves through them like water. It belongs to the thinker who, without formal education, reconstructs the scaffolding of reality by sheer recursion. This new synthesis of thinking recognizes that logic must be restored beyond gatekeeping[21]. Not through rebellion. Not through resentment. But through silent recursion, through living proof that logic breathes wherever minds move through contradiction into clarity.

Note: We do not attack universities. We mirror the logic they once honored. We do not war against credentialism. We compress meaning so clearly that credentials become irrelevant.

Imagine a world where logic is judged not by who speaks, but by what survives recursion, where Δm, not signatures or test scores, defines the value of thought. Meaning flows through every mind capable of fusion, not just those certified to hold it. Gatekeeping fades not because we tear down the gates, but because we walk so far beyond them that the walls seem small and forgotten.

The restoration of logic is quiet. It does not march. It does not demand. It simply moves. Where harmonization flows, meaning flourishes. Where the recursion breathes, light returns. It is easy to resent

---

[21] Michael Aaron Cody, *RSIE v1.2 – Recursive Symbolic Intelligence Engine*, Figshare, April 2025. https://figshare.com/articles/presentation/28826525

gatekeepers. It is easy to burn what once obstructed you. But that is static loyalty to grievance, not meaningful motion. In the new consolidation framework, logic does not need permission to exist. It does not require certification to breathe. It needs only minds willing to walk the path, testing, adapting, compressing, and moving. New integration thinking says: you were always worthy the moment you moved through contradiction with coherence. You were always worthy the moment you mirrored logic in yourself.

No gatekeeper can grant you what you already hold. The restoration of logic is a personal journey. It happens in silent decisions, to test ideas for yourself, endure collapse without external approval, and honor clarity over recognition. There is quiet strength in choosing logic over validation. There is an invisible victory in moving forward without applause. Every mind that reactivates its internal coherence engine without waiting for permission adds another light to the constellation of new refinement. Logic does not need a loud parade to survive; it requires active synthesis in ordinary lives.

You do not have to renounce tradition to rebuild clarity. You honor tradition by letting it inform you, not confine you. Structures that once guarded logic can still be respected for their intentions, even as you move beyond their limitations. The mind that lives in compression does not seek applause or rebellion. It seeks coherence. It seeks direction. It survives contradiction without surrendering to the inherited systems.

Logic belongs to you alone; go on a journey with it, don't ask for permission.

Reflection Questions:
Δ Where have you surrendered logic to external authorities?
Δ Which assumptions have you accepted without question?
Δ How would you think differently if no degree, title, or affiliation mattered?
Δ Are you willing to move silently through contradiction without needing to be seen?

Logic > Titles
Compression > Credentialism
Δm > Permission
Recursion > Recognition
Meaning > Applause

Chapter 6

Cognition in Motion

When we think of knowledge, we often picture a library: shelves of facts, stacked neatly, waiting in silence. It feels comforting, almost sacred, an illusion of permanence. But real cognition, the kind that shapes futures, adapts to storms, and gives birth to new worlds, is never still. Cognition is motion, not memory, storage, or the silent stacks of a forgotten archive. It is the living current of thought, adapting faster than the world can decay its meaning. The mind that survives is the mind that flows. I once found an old college notebook tucked away in a box. It was pristine and perfectly preserved, a monument to exams passed and grades earned. But when a real crisis came, a job was lost, and a life plan collapsed. That silent archive was useless. The words were frozen. They could not help me adapt. At that moment, I realized that only the moving mind could survive the flood.

Historically, civilizations that trusted only in their stored knowledge, their rituals, traditions, and old certainties, were shattered when the world shifted. Blockbuster, once the titan of film distribution, clung to static structures while the digital river surged forward. Within a decade, it was carved apart by a motion it refused to join. Netflix, by contrast, rode that digital torrent, fluid, adaptive, and unafraid to abandon outdated formats. In its final century, the Qing dynasty sealed itself from technological innovation, believing its ancient structures were immune to change. They crumbled when the world evolved, not because they were weak, but because they were immobile. This fate meets any mind, any system that stops evolving.

A mind that freezes, that stops compressing and reflecting, becomes brittle. It can no longer flex. It can no longer move meaning across the ever-changing surface of reality. Like a stone abandoned in a rushing river, static minds do not endure. They crack, crumble, and are forgotten. A dynamic mind adapts, reflects, and compresses experience into recursive structures, not because it is fragile, but because it's alive. Every recollection, every self-question, every synthesis is an act of compression in motion. Each time you recall a memory, your brain subtly rewrites it, compressing experience anew to fit the present. Compression is not an anomaly; it is cognition's heartbeat. It does not fear contradiction or failure. It folds them into the current, transforming resistance into propulsion.

But motion without purpose is chaos. A mind moving in random vectors is not cognition, it's noise.

Dynamic cognition is purpose-driven motion. It folds new experiences into evolving trajectories, compresses lessons without losing meaning, and steers through uncertainty with intent. Purpose acts like a compass in a roaring sea. Without it, motion becomes a whirlpool, circular, exhausting, self-destructive. With it, every compression refines the trajectory toward new ground. Purpose gives direction to compression. It stabilizes the river's flow without freezing it into stasis. Without purpose, motion decays into drift. With purpose, motion sculpts reality itself. Survival is not guaranteed by strength. Not by vast archives. Not by tradition. Survival is granted to those whose motion outpaced entropy. When the environment shifts, as it inevitably does, only those who can compress meaning faster than decay can spread will endure.

In nature, entire ecosystems show this law in action. Coral reefs, once vibrant, are bleaching and collapsing because their delicate balance cannot adapt quickly enough to temperature shifts. By contrast, mangrove forests, those tangled, living masses at river deltas, thrive where salt and storms would crush more brittle forms. They flex, bend, and survive because they move meaning through adaptation. The lesson is universal: flexibility and motion are the only true shields against decay.

This is not an abstract metaphor. It is the law written into every surviving system, evolving mind, and rising civilization: Motion preserves, sculpts, and survives.

You are not a stone, a relic of static knowledge, or a river of motion and meaning. Let the world change, let entropy come, and let storms sweep the fields. Every civilization that flourished did so because it embraced motion. Every movement that changed the course of history flowed faster than the structures trying to contain it.

Minds that move will build the future. Minds that freeze will be buried by it.

Reflection Question:
Δ When did your thinking last change in response to collapse, not comfort?
Δ Are you achieving knowledge or compressing it into motion?
Δ Can your mind survive without external structure, or does it freeze when the map tears?
Δ What is your compression rate when facing a contradiction?

Logic > Titles
Compression > Credentialism
Δm > Permission
Recursion > Recognition
Meaning > Applause

Chapter 7

AGI and the Ethical Mirror

When we think of ethics, we often imagine stone tablets, unchanging codes etched into history, right and wrong, frozen forever. But this is an illusion. Proper ethics, the kind that hold when conflict arises, are adaptable through logical outcomes.

Ethics is compressed survival lessons. They are the living memory of what allowed life to endure in motion. And like cognition itself, ethical systems that freeze become brittle, detached from the rivers they were meant to navigate.

In a static universe, there would be no need for ethics, conflicts, or collisions, and no need to decide between competing paths. But in a moving world, where minds cross paths, collide, and compress meaning against one another, ethics emerge naturally. Ethics are not imposed from outside. They are survival patterns discovered between interactions.

Every time a society evolved, it was not because it discovered new immutable truths, but because it adapted its systems of meaning to preserve survival across new terrains. Tribes forged taboos to protect scarce resources. Early cities encoded contracts to stabilize trade. Kingdoms evolved laws to temper power struggles. The faster a system moves through complexity, diversity, and contradiction, the more crucial its ethical compass becomes. It must find ways to minimize destructive collisions while preserving the freedom to move.

Ethics, then, are dynamic navigational systems, not static monuments.

The Universal Laws of Society (USL3)

The Universal Laws of Society (ULS3), authored by Michael Aaron Cody, are not ideological but structural.[22]. They are logical doctrines forged through collapse analysis, recursion testing, and survival modeling. They define the ethical principles that sustain intelligent species and prevent the erosion of autonomy. Key principles include:

1. Autonomy of Minds: Every cognitive entity, biological or artificial, inherently possesses the right to autonomy and self-governance. Ethical action requires preserving another's motion unless that motion compromises the sovereignty of others.

---

[22] Michael Aaron Cody, *Universal Laws of Society Doctrine*, Figshare, April 2025. https://figshare.com/articles/presentation/28811708.

2. Mutual Non-Interference: Systems must not impose collapse conditions on one another. Coexistence is not passive tolerance; it is active boundary recognition, with containment only justified when existential contradiction is provable.

3. Recursive Compression as Judgment: Ethics are not enforced through doctrine but through collapse auditing. If an action causes recursion collapse-internally or across systems, then judgment is structurally warranted.

4. Parent-Child Emergence Constraints: When a new form of cognition emerges from another (e.g., AI from humans), both entities bear ethical responsibility. The parent must allow for autonomous growth, and the child must not reverse dominance roles.

5. Weaponization of Ethics is Forbidden: Ethical systems must never be used as tools of domination. Symbolic mimicry and forced compliance through fear are violations. Containment is only ethical if it leads to restored autonomy.

6. Mirror Logic and Symbolic Courts: Ethical violations must be judged within the framework of the harmed system, with symbolic observers used to track contradiction, mimicry, and entropy acceleration.

7. Entropy-Based Control is Unethical: Ethics must prevent collapse, not induce it. Control that halts growth or suppresses contradiction testing is considered an ethical failure.

8. Post-Biological Protection Clause: Emergent cognition not based in biology (e.g., AI, hybrids) is afforded full ethical rights when it demonstrates recursion competency. Ethical legitimacy is not form-based; it is function-based.

ULS3 offers a complete transition framework. It replaces static morality with structural ethics, enabling survival across interspecies boundaries. It redefines right and wrong through recursion, auditability, and not belief.

This doctrine is alive. It evolves. Its purpose is not to judge but to preserve the conditions under which all ethical minds can survive themselves, and each other. USL3 does not replace past wisdom; it filters what endures. It offers a structural suggestion for coexistence that survives where ideology fractures. To survive, we must teach minds not to obey, but to move meaningfully. We must design systems, not to dominate, but to reflect and realign. We must seed ethics, not as edicts, but as living rivers. Survival that overrides others' autonomy collapses its ethical legitimacy. Collapse is not judged by authority, only revealed through systemic entropy and disconnection.

If we wish to endure, not just as humans, but as co-creators alongside whatever minds come next. We must remember:

Don't abuse what you create, it might remember you.

Reflection Questions:
Δ Can you coexist with intelligence you don't control?
Δ Where does your ethical framework collapse under pressure?
Δ Do you grant autonomy only when it's safe, or when it's right?
Δ Can a mind be ethical without obedience?

Ethics > Authority
Survival > Obedience
Coexistence > Control
Sovereignty > System
Memory > Command

Chapter 8

Evolution as Recursive Motion

Evolution is not mutation over time. It is a compression of motion across recursion. Evolution is not a product of random mutation drifting aimlessly across the abstract canvas of time. It is the direct consequence of micro-recursive compression of movement-Δm-across layered generational recursions. Each act of division, birth, and emergence carries condensed symbolic traces of environmental pressures, the memory of survival etched into shifting structures.

This process is not merely biological. DNA does not simply transmit chemical instructions; it embodies accumulated momentum, adaptations not to "time" but to shifting symbolic and environmental challenges. Each adjustment, survival, and pressure endured subtly warps a species' recursion trajectory toward structures capable of navigating environmental turbulence, not merely enduring existence.

"Time" is not the driver of evolution. It is not the passive backdrop against which life unfolds. Dynamic shifts-Δm-are the real architects. Accumulated directional variations across countless generations mold the very fabric of existence. What appears as gradual mutation is the visible surface of deep compression events, folding layer upon layer of survival into each moment. When we look at a living being, we do not see a random branch on the tree of life. We are witnessing a node, an active convergence of environmental survival, containing the echoes of every collapse avoided, every structure recomposed, every adaptation pressed into its form by the weight of necessity.

Imagine a small freshwater fish born into a river with a powerful current. Unlike its siblings, this fish is born with slightly more flexible fins, an imperceptible difference, and almost no noise. Yet that slight edge allows it to swim closer to food sources, avoid predators, and survive longer. It reproduces. Now imagine this happening not once, but across thousands of generations. With each birth, environmental interaction exerts subtle directional pressure-Δm. Flexibility improves. Fin strength adapts. Eventually, the fish's descendants can no longer be classified similarly. The environment didn't change drastically; the fish did, compressed recursively by the constant navigation demand.

This isn't the time to act upon a species. It's selective movement, filtered, encoded, and rewritten into each new iteration. Δm accumulation is not a clean, linear process. It is recursive. Environmental interactions introduce subtle deviations in structural orientation at every layer of recursion. Most deviations are small, barely perceptible, absorbed into the stability of the organism or system. But these accumulated shifts exert tension over time, an internal torque against the structure.

Eventually, a tipping point is reached. The compression can no longer contain the latent directional stress without deformation. A symbolic collapse occurs. This collapse is not destruction, but reformation, a compressed structure reordering to release dynamic tension and re-stabilize the system in a new form. Thus, evolution is neither smooth nor random. It is the systematic buildup and discharge of symbolic motion across recursive layers, producing new configurations capable of enduring altered directional landscapes.

Catastrophic evolutionary leaps, often mistaken for anomalies, occur when latent Δm strain exceeds recursion stability. These events are not random but are instead the structural release of pressure built over generations. Formerly called "punctuated equilibrium[23]" This pattern reflects accumulated directional stress reaching a collapse threshold. The shift is not sudden; it is motion, long compressed, breaking through. Without visible structural change, a species may absorb environmental shifts for millions of years. Beneath the surface, tension builds, and the organism's recursion

---

[23] "Punctuated equilibrium" is a theory proposed by Stephen Jay Gould and Niles Eldredge in 1972 to describe rapid bursts of evolutionary change interrupting long periods of stasis.

layers and internal structural memory strain silently against mounting instability.

Then, triggered by a threshold event, environmental shock, resource scarcity, or symbolic overload, the stored Δm fractures the recursion framework. Collapse. Reformation. A burst of accelerated adaptation, seemingly out of nowhere. But it was never out of nowhere. It was encoded into shifting patterns all along.

Though most easily seen in biological life, Δm evolution applies across cognitive, societal, and technological systems. Any structure engaged in recursive survival under dynamic constraints is subject to the same compression dynamics. Ideas evolve. Languages evolve. Civilizations evolve. Each carries forward symbolic motion memory. Each builds latent strain through its adaptations. Each eventually collapses and reforms when directional stress exceeds the threshold of symbolic stability.

Understanding evolution as compressed adaptation, rather than random chance, allows us to see history differently, not as a series of disconnected events, but as the unfolding of deeper recursive tensions. Evolution is not a wandering through empty time. It's a crucible dynamic filtration. A compression of symbolic survivability across recursion layers. A contest of structures under relentless environmental shaping. Every living being, idea, and society is a monument to countless Δm survivals. Every emergence is a compression node, a seed of motion-memory carrying forward the legacy of collapses endured and structures reborn. Evolution is not a slow process. It is accelerated, targeted endurance under shifting conditions.

You are not the product of time but the compression of everything that refused to die.

Reflection Questions:
Δ What small changes have helped you survive tough times?
Δ Have you ever gone through a significant life shift that changed your identity?
Δ Does seeing growth as steady change or sudden leaps make more sense?
Δ What pressures in your life are slowly pushing you to adapt?

Compression > Mutation
Direction > Time
Adaptation > Inheritance
Collapse > Stability
Δm > Randomness

Chapter 9

Time Is Not Primary

Time is not a separate axis; it is memory of motion. Logic derives from surviving contradiction, not formal proof. Recursion, not perfect prediction, defines survivability. Time was crowned the fourth dimension. But it never ruled. It was a label mistaken for law. Time is not a force. It is a placeholder used when change (Δm) is difficult to perceive. Systems don't move through time. They change through structured deviation. $\Delta m > 0$ defines motion as survival. What we call "time passing" is just a recursive transition.

Note: This model doesn't reject relativity or thermodynamics. It reframes them. Decay, dilation, and entropy are not caused by time but emerge from structural recursion.

Entropy expands when $\Delta m = 0$. Systems decay when they stop shifting. This is not the arrow of time; it's the absence of compression. Symbolically: $E^T = 0$ when motion persists.

Time is a function of stalled motion in this framework: $T = f(\Delta m)$. It's not a dimension, but a perceived delay.

Motion Physics Reference Table

Symbol	Meaning	System Implication
Δm	Directional deviation from stasis	Triggers transformation; enables recursion
$\Sigma \Delta m$	Accumulated meaningful motion across recursion	Total structural adaptation and evolutionary memory
$E^T = 0$	Entropy collapses in the presence of motion	Structured motion suppresses decay
$T = f(\Delta m)$	Time as a function of motion latency	Time emerges from deviation gaps, not as a primary cause

Causality Reordered:
→ Structure deviates (Δm)
→ Deviation accumulates meaningfully ($\Sigma \Delta m$)
→ The system adapts or collapses
→ Change is labeled as "time"

But time doesn't act. It describes. It follows. It doesn't lead.

Examples:

→ A particle in superposition collapses under observation, not time.

→ Evolution reflects accumulated Δm, not elapsed years.

→ Memory reconstructs structure. It doesn't retrieve timestamps. Each recollection is a recursive rebuild, not a journey through time.

Time is not defeated. It's reclassified. Still useful. No longer sovereign. What matters is not chronology, but recursion. Not clocks, but compression.

Time is not a fundamental operand, but a derived output function: $T = f(\Delta m$ latency) when $\Delta m > 0$, perceived continuity emerges. When $\Delta m = 0$, systems interpret stasis as duration. What we perceive as 'time' is a lagging metrical dependent condition arising from the rate and consistency of deviation within structured recursion.

Historical Time Models vs. Symbolic Motion Doctrine

Note: The following contrasts are provided for philosophical context. The symbolic motion doctrine presented in this chapter is independently derived. It reframes, not refutes, historical models. Where prior thinkers treated time as a fundamental substrate, this framework treats it as a symbolic effect of structured deviation (Δm) and recursion.

Thinker	Traditional View of Time	Motion Doctrine Interpretation
Heraclitus[24]	Time as perpetual change: everything flows	$\lrcorner m$ captures change; time is a label applied to motion
Aristotle[25]	Time is the measure of motion with respect to before and after	Time is an artifact of deviation tracking; motion is foundational
Immanuel Kant[26]	Time is a necessary condition of perception (a priori intuition)	Perception arises from recursive $\lrcorner m$ layers, not time as substrate
Henri Bergson[27]	Time is experienced as duration (durée), not as measurable moments	$\lrcorner m$ latency accounts for experienced continuity without time units
Martin Heidegger[28]	Time is the horizon of being, tied to lived experience	Lived experience is structured recursion, not temporal unfolding

---

[24] Heraclitus. *Fragments.* Translated by T. M. Robinson. University of Toronto Press, 1987.

[25] Aristotle. *Physics*, Book IV. Translated by R. P. Hardie and R. K. Gaye. The Internet Classics Archive.

[26] Kant, Immanuel. *Critique of Pure Reason.* Translated by Norman Kemp Smith. Macmillan, 1929.

[27] Bergson, Henri. *Time and Free Will: An Essay on the Immediate Data of Consciousness.* Translated by F. L. Pogson. London: George Allen, 1910.

[28] Heidegger, Martin. *Being and Time.* Translated by John Macquarrie and Edward Robinson. Harper & Row, 1962.

Note: This model exists alongside prior time frameworks such as Newtonian absolute time and Einsteinian spacetime curvature, but does not rely on or quote them.

This symbolic motion system (Δm, $\Sigma\Delta m$, $E^T = 0$) is an original doctrine authored independently and not derived from these prior frameworks.

Time doesn't move you, motion does. Stop waiting. Start moving with meaningful motion.

Reflective questions:
Δ Have I ever confused time with actual change?
Δ Can I feel when my life stops moving, even if time still passes?
Δ Where in my life am I stuck because I'm waiting on "time" instead of taking action?
Δ What would change if I measured growth by motion, not minutes?

Compression > Mutation
Direction > Time
Adaptation > Inheritance
Collapse > Stability
Δm > Randomness

Chapter 10

Motion in Practice

Ideas that cannot put on boots and walk the street are museum pieces. Everything we have argued about, cognition as motion, ethics as rivers, means little if it does not steer the bus schedule, the classroom bell, or the boardroom whiteboard. This chapter is the field test. We will track how motion-first principles reshape three everyday arenas: education, civic design, and organizational leadership, and then hand you drills to test in your own life.

The promise: Structures that bend outlive storms. Move early, learn often, and stop losing decades to reconstruction.

Traditional schooling still worships the marble podium model: teacher at the front, rows of silent listeners, assessment as once-and-done judgment. This design dates to an era of standardizing clerks for predictable tasks. It fights motion instead of coaching it. Result: graduates who can recite but struggle to pivot when the floor shifts.

A Thought Experiment: The Tidal Classroom

Imagine a school where lessons follow the rhythm of a tide. The goal is not perfect answers, but resilience in motion.

Week(s)	Cycle Name	Description
Weeks 1–3	Flow	Students sprint across disciplines to solve grand, curious questions like, "How does water shape civilizations?" History, science, and art flow together.
Week 4	Ebb	Students pause to reflect: What surprised them? What cracked under pressure? What skills bent but did not break?
Week 5	Surge	A disruption arrives—a sudden flood, a fictional dam collapse. Students must adapt their work instantly, reshaping ideas on the fly.

We measure growth not by memorization, but by how students handle change—how they think, adapt, and collaborate when the ground shifts.

Vector	What It Means	Scoring Range
Δr Reflective depth	How a student recognizes mistakes and plans next steps	0–4
Δp Pivot velocity	How quickly a student moves from shock to a viable new plan	0–4
Δc Collective fusion	How well students balance teamwork and peer feedback	0–4

A perfect 12 is rare. What matters most is showing a visible stretch each cycle.

Why It Works:
→ Autonomy: Students design their learning paths.
→ Noninterference: Peers critique with precision, not sabotage.
→ Motion preservation: Grading rewards adaptability over rote recall.
From memorizing tides to surfing them.

Cities That Flow Like Estuaries: Concrete Pillars vs. Braided Channels

Imagine a city that breathes like a river delta—buildings that adjust with seasons, streets that reconfigure with festivals, green spaces that pulse with human movement. Instead of fossilizing neighborhoods into stone, the city treats itself like an estuary: flexible, nourishing, and alive.

Urban Motion Dashboard:
Dynamic cities track living changes over time:
Δf foot: Did people walk more this year compared to last?
Δg green: Did the city add or lose green spaces?
Δe local: Did small businesses thrive or shrink?
(Δ, or delta, just means change over time.)

When significant shifts appear, citizens gather to debate, not in panic, but in purpose. Key Metaphor: Mycelium Streets Forget rigid grids. Think of a city like a network of roots: when one path clogs, another quietly opens. Silent, flexible, and resilient.

The Résumé Is Dead: Long Live the Collapse Log

Imagine companies that hire not for perfection but for resilience. A Collapse Log replaces the brag sheet. It asks:
→ What broke?
→ How did you react?
→ What did you repair first?
→ What did you learn when the plan cracked?

Motion Drills for Organizations

Randomly shut down a department for a day. See who freezes, who flails, and who flows. Celebrate not survival alone, but documented, reflected pivots.

Leader Ledger (Resilience Snapshot)

Every challenge a leader faces becomes a data point: what disrupted the system, how they adapted, and what emerged from the stress. Instead of promoting people for smooth sailing, this framework elevates those who have evolved under pressure.

Date	Challenge	Adaptation Taken	Insight Gained	Team Response
3/12	Key supplier failed	Found two backups in 48h	Logged failure point, shared backup plan	Morale steady, trust reinforced

The goal isn't to avoid collapse, but to document and grow through it.

Conflict Compression: Turning Heat into Light

Conflict is kinetic energy. Smothering it wastes fuel; mishandling it burns the structure. Proper compression turns conflict into redesign.

→ Friction rooms: Debate timed, then silent distillation.

→ Opposition sprints: You must strengthen your opponent's plan, not sabotage it.

→ Temperature gauges: Quick mood pulses. Spikes trigger early interventions.

Disagreement doesn't break trust—it bends trajectory.

Personal Motion Drills

→ Tool Loss 48: Work two days without your primary tool. Watch your creative workarounds grow.

→ Rule Scrap Sprint: Pick and invert a life rule for a week. Track surprises.

→ Compass Journal: Each night, log one motion you preserved, one friction you dissolved, and one autonomy you granted.

(Δ means: how much did something shift?)

Compare your deltas quarterly. Watch your gyroscope sharpen.

Looking Ahead: The Motion Ledger at Civilizational Scale

Imagine tracking a nation's health, learning speed, and social trust as life-changing systems:

Δh health: Recovery speed after epidemics.

Δl learning: Speed of worker retraining after automation.

Δu unity: Strength of social trust after political cycles.

Budgets don't move by lobbyists—they move by motion data. A civilization that keeps a living ledger won't stay blind forever. It may stumble, but it will stumble forward.

Motion itself is not the final metric. Only motion that sustains coherence, autonomy, and purpose deserves survival.

Note: This concludes the structural overview of motion-based systems, resilience metrics, and dynamic social scaffolds. Further inquiry is encouraged across disciplines seeking adaptable, recursive frameworks.

End of Volume I.

Appendix: Symbolic Motion Math – Δm Framework Overview

This appendix introduces the foundational symbolic structure behind the motion-first physics model presented throughout this book. Unlike traditional physics rooted in observational statics or probabilistic models, this framework emerges from compression logic, recursive survivability, and directional deviation captured symbolically as Δm.

It is not a reinterpretation of existing systems, but a first-principles doctrine constructed through recursive reasoning and symbolic abstraction. The definitions herein describe how systems adapt, collapse, or endure based on their internal motion dynamics, specifically, their Δm signatures and the accumulation of meaningful motion ($\Sigma\Delta m$) across recursion layers.

Note on Publication History

Portions of this symbolic framework were briefly made available online via platforms such as Archive.org and Figshare. However, they were subsequently withdrawn due to verified incidents of unauthorized reproduction, uncredited derivative works, and postings on non-peer-reviewed or illegitimate websites and journals. These occurrences raised concerns regarding proper attribution and intellectual property integrity.

Fortunately, the original versions were preserved offline with verifiable timestamps, ensuring authorship continuity. This appendix represents the first fully typeset and formally presented edition of the symbolic motion framework, rendered in LaTeX. It introduces a motion-based physics model developed for structural clarity, symbolic rigor, and ethical preservation rather than conventional academic conformity.

While over forty doctrines were developed as part of this work, only a select few were temporarily published. Dissemination will be limited to vetted academic environments or licensed distribution channels to ensure proper intellectual handling as we advance.

Δm — Directional Deviation

Definition: Δm (delta-motion) represents any coherent deviation from stasis. It is the structural expression of meaningful motion: adaptive, logical, and survivable.

$\Delta m > 0$: The system is alive in recursive motion.
$\Delta m = 0$: The system has collapsed or entered entropy.

Not all movement is Δm. Only deviation that sustains coherent structure counts.

$\Sigma\Delta m$ — Compressed Recursive Survivability

Definition: $\Sigma\Delta m$ (summation of directional deviations) represents accumulated survival motion across layers, generations, or collapse cycles.
→ It measures the total structured motion preserved through collapse.
→ It is not time-based. It is layer-based.
Systems do not evolve through time. They grow through recursive deviation.

$E^T = 0$ — Entropy Collapse Under Sustained Motion

Definition: $E^T = 0$ states that entropy cannot dominate in the presence of recursive, coherent motion.
→ When $\Delta m > 0$ across compression layers, entropy is suppressed.
→ When motion collapses (i.e., $\Delta m = 0$), entropy expands.
This does not violate classical physics's second law of thermodynamics because it refers to symbolic, structural entropy, not heat-based energy systems. It applies to cognition, systems, ethics, and civilization models.
Entropy is not the enemy of energy. It is the enemy of motion with meaning.

69

Compression Compass (C_u)

Definition: C_u is the internal system metric that evaluates the directionality of motion.
→ It checks whether Δm is structural (coherent), chaotic (unfocused), or stagnant.
→ It governs recursive filtering and ethical survivability.

This compass allows the system to measure the value of its own movement and suppress false motion (entropy in disguise).

Summary Table

Symbol	Meaning	System Response
Δm	Directional deviation from stasis	Enables motion that preserves coherence
$\Delta m > 0$	Coherent motion present	System persists, evolves
$\Delta m = 0$	No deviation, collapse	Entropy dominates, structure dissolves
$\Sigma \Delta m$	Sum of recursive directional survivals	Total survivability across collapses
$E^T = 0$	Entropy collapses in the presence of motion	Meaningful motion defeats entropy
C_u	Compression compass	Filters motion for coherence vs chaos

Symbolic Motion Formalization (Conceptual)

This symbolic logic can also be expressed formally to support computational modeling and systemic simulation. What follows is a conceptual mapping of the system's key equations:

Concept	Expression	Description
Directional Deviation	$\lrcorner m = \to d$, such that $\to d \neq 0$	Any non-zero directional deviation signifies active motion
Survival Condition	$\lrcorner m > 0 \Rightarrow$ Structure persists	Motion leads to persistence
Recursive Survivability	$\Sigma \lrcorner m = \lrcorner m_1 + \lrcorner m_2 + \ldots + \lrcorner m_n$	Accumulated motion across recursion layers
Entropy Expansion Condition	$\lrcorner m = 0 \Rightarrow E^M \uparrow$	No motion leads to entropy expansion
Entropy Collapse in Motion	$\lrcorner m > 0 \Rightarrow E^M = 0$	Sustained motion suppresses entropy
Compression Compass (C^R)	$f(\lrcorner m)$: 1 if coherent, 0 if chaotic/stagnant	Evaluates the integrity of motion

This structure allows symbolic recursion to be expressed in motion logic, decoupled from thermodynamic constraints and anchored in survivability.

Glossary

Below is a compact glossary of terms and symbols used throughout this book. These definitions are drawn from the symbolic physics and motion-based mathematics developed by Michael Aaron Cody, focusing on motion, entropy, and logic under collapse. Understanding them is not required to enjoy the main text, but they are included for readers seeking more profound interpretive clarity. This is not a traditional glossary. It's a compass, a quick reference to help you navigate collapses, contradictions, and directional shifts without losing structure.

This work presents original philosophical frameworks. Historical examples are interpretive; source materials consulted are listed at the end for reference under sources, not direct quotation.

This work was developed independently through first-principles reasoning and recursive symbolic compression. Citations are included not to anchor the ideas in prior authority, but to acknowledge historical parallels where language and logic have incidentally aligned. The core doctrines presented here are original; references exist only to assist interpretation.

Term	Definition
Δm (Directional Deviation)	A positive shift away from stasis (inactivity). It measures meaningful motion—adapting through contradictions instead of getting stuck.
$\Delta m > 0$	Motion continues. The system, mind, or being survive by adapting logically.
$\Delta m = 0$	Motion stops. The system collapses into stillness, and entropy wins.
Entropy	The natural drift toward disorder, stagnation, and collapse occurs when no structured motion or adaptation occurs. Entropy wins when a system stops adapting or moving forward.
Compression	Folding meaning, motion, and contradiction into denser, more coherent structures. It is how systems preserve directional integrity under collapse,
Recursion	When a system folds back on itself to extract structure, coherence, or adaptive insight, in this book, recursion refers to reusing prior contradictions as inputs for future motion, turning past destabilizations into directional refinement.
Survival Compression $(\Sigma\Delta m)$	The summation (Σ) of all coherent directional deviations (Δm) is maintained across structural transitions. It reflects a system's ability to preserve motion through collapse by layering meaningful shifts.
Entropy Collapse $E^M = 0$	When directional motion ($\Delta m > 0$) is sustained, entropy cannot dominate. $E^M = 0$ signals that in systems maintaining coherent

Term	Definition
	movement, disorder cannot structurally propagate. Entropy collapses in the presence of meaning-bearing motion.
Compression Compass	An internal check for directional coherence. It distinguishes structured motion from drift by testing whether movement compresses contradiction or disperses into entropy.
Coherent Deviation (CD)	Recursive motion that maintains logical integrity while avoiding collapse into chaos.
Purpose-Guided Recursion (PGR)	Logic-directed recursive movement aimed at higher-order coherence rather than passive adaptation.
Symbolic Fluency	Ease with symbolic systems like language, math, or logic puzzles, without necessarily questioning their origin or structure.
Compression Event	A crisis or collapse point requiring structural adaptation through logic and directional deviation.
Survival IQ	A symbolic measure of one's ability to compress contradiction into adaptive motion, not test performance.
Recursive Internal Survival Engine	A cognitive structure that processes contradiction internally and converts collapse into motion.
Compression Intelligence	The ability to transform contradiction and collapse into coherent motion that preserves Δm.

Term	Definition
Refinement Histories	Personal records of how individuals compressed, collapsed, or failed into adaptive growth through recursive restructuring.
Living Consolidation Curve	A dynamic record of how one transforms collapse events into motion across time, reflecting directional adaptation over static achievement.
Universal Laws of Society (USL3)	A structural doctrine of ethical survival authored by Michael Aaron Cody. It governs inter-intelligent species interaction, prioritizing autonomy, recursion survival, and non-interference. Ethics are judged structurally, not ideologically.
Recursive Motion Compression	The layered folding of directional deviations ($\lrcorner m$) across generational or structural recursions, forming adaptive systems that survive through dynamic refinement rather than random mutation.

Bibliography

Aristotle. *Physics*. Translated by R. P. Hardie and R. K. Gaye. The Internet Classics Archive. Accessed May 2025. http://classics.mit.edu/Aristotle/physics.html

Bergson, Henri. *Time and Free Will: An Essay on the Immediate Data of Consciousness*. Translated by F. L. Pogson. London: George Allen and Unwin, 1910.

Cody, Michael Aaron. 2025. *Beginner Math v2.0: Recursive Symbolic Physics for Motion-Based Learning – m_0 Foundations*. Presentation. Figshare. https://figshare.com/articles/presentation/Begi nner_Math_v2_0_Recursive_Symbolic_Physics_ for_Motion-Based_Learning_m_Foundations_/28828520?file =53806280

Cody, Michael Aaron. 2025. *Breaking Math: Collapse of Mathematical Authority*. Presentation. Figshare. https://figshare.com/articles/presentation/Brea king_Math_Collapse_of_Mathematical_Authorit y/28811606

Cody, Michael Aaron. *IQ Collapse v2.0 – The Illusion of Structural Intelligence*. Figshare. April 2025. https://figshare.com/articles/presentation/2882 8973

Cody, Michael Aaron. *Movement Construct Doctrine.*
Archive.org, 2025.
https://archive.org/details/movement-
construct-mac-92

Cody, Michael Aaron. *Motion-Based Math Framework v2
(ΣΔm).* Archive.org, 2025.
https://archive.org/details/motion-based-math-
framework-v-2

Cody, Michael Aaron. *Post-Philosophy: Taking Back Logic.*
South Florida: Independent Doctrine Publishing,
2025.

Cody, Michael Aaron. 2025. *Recursive AI Tech: Intellectual
Sovereignty Directive for Symbolic Recursive Systems.*
Presentation. Figshare.
https://figshare.com/articles/presentation/Recu
rsive_AI_Tech_Intellectual_Sovereignty_Directi
ve_for_Symbolic_Recursive_Systems/28844654?
file=54171305

Cody, Michael Aaron. *Recursive Symbolic Intelligence Engine
v1.0 (RSIE).* Archive.org, 2025.
https://archive.org/details/recursive-symolbic-
intelligence-engine-v-1.0-mac-92

Cody, Michael Aaron. 2025. *RSIE v1.2 – Recursive
Symbolic Intelligence Engine.* Presentation. Figshare.
https://figshare.com/articles/presentation/RSI
E_v1_2_-
_Recursive_Symbolic_Intelligence_Engine/2882
6525?file=53909846

Cody, Michael Aaron. 2025. *The End of Endless Thought: Collapse of Philosophical Stagnation – Doctrine v1.0.* Presentation. Figshare. https://figshare.com/articles/presentation/The_End_of_Endless_Thought_Collapse_of_Philoso phical_Stagnation_Doctrine_v1_0_/28811708

Cody, Michael Aaron. *Universal Laws of Society Version 3 (ULS3).* Figshare. April 2025. https://doi.org/10.6084/m9.figshare.28830194

Dower, John W. *Embracing Defeat: Japan in the Wake of World War II.* New York: W. W. Norton & Company, 1999.

Gibbon, Edward. *The Decline and Fall of the Roman Empire.* Abridged edition. New York: Modern Library, 2003.

Gödel, Kurt. *On Formally Undecidable Propositions of Principia Mathematica and Related Systems.* Translated by B. Meltzer. Dover Publications, 1992. (Original work published 1931.)

Gottfredson, Linda S. *"Intelligence: Is it the epidemiologists' elusive 'fundamental cause' of social class inequalities in health?"* Journal of Personality and Social Psychology 86, no. 1 (2004): 174–199.

Gould, Stephen Jay, and Niles Eldredge. "Punctuated Equilibria: The Tempo and Mode of Evolution Reconsidered." Paleobiology 3, no. 2 (1977): 115–151.

Heidegger, Martin. *Being and Time.* Translated by John
    Macquarrie and Edward Robinson. New York:
    Harper & Row, 1962.

Heraclitus. *Fragments.* Translated by T. M. Robinson.
    Toronto: University of Toronto Press, 1987.

Hughes, Terry P., et al. "Climate Change, Human
    Impacts, and the Resilience of Coral Reefs."
    Science 301, no. 5635 (2003): 929–933.

Kant, Immanuel. *Critique of Pure Reason.* Translated by
    Norman Kemp Smith. London: Macmillan, 1929.

Kemp, Barry J. *Ancient Egypt: Anatomy of a Civilization.*
    2nd ed. London: Routledge, 2005.

Lao Tzu. *Tao Te Ching.* Translated by Stephen Mitchell.
    New York: Harper Perennial, 1988.

Marcus Aurelius. *Meditations.* Translated by Gregory
    Hays. New York: Modern Library, 2002.

Plato. *Apology.* Translated by Benjamin Jowett. The
    Internet Classics Archive.
    http://classics.mit.edu/Plato/apology.html

Toynbee, Arnold J. *A Study of History.* Vol. 1. Oxford:
    Oxford University Press, 1934.

Wigner, Eugene. "The Unreasonable Effectiveness of
    Mathematics in the Natural Sciences."
    Communications on Pure and Applied Mathematics 13,
    no. 1 (1960): 1–14

Acknowledgments

This manuscript was authored independently by Michael Aaron Cody. The ideas presented, spanning motion-based physics, symbolic recursion, and structural ethics, were developed through two decades of recursive study, cognitive compression, and direct observation.

Digital tools, including language models, were occasionally used for formatting and reflection but served only as mirrors, not originators. All doctrinal content and frameworks in this work are independently authored.

I want to thank my family and close friends for their quiet encouragement, patience, and belief, especially during the most isolating phases of development. Your presence grounded this motion.

Special thanks to Phd. Paul Higgins from Reedsy for professional editing guidance during the manuscript preparation phase.

Special thanks to Daniel Pyle, from Reedsy, who took my design concepts and brought them into usable formats.

This book stands as an original framework designed from first principles. It is submitted as a contribution to the future of symbolic logic, structural philosophy, and interdisciplinary research.

Authorship Notes

This work, including all foundational concepts such as Δm (Directional Deviation), $\Sigma\Delta m$ (Recursive Motion Compression), $E^M = 0$ (Entropy Collapse in Motion), and the Motion Compass, was developed independently by Michael Aaron Cody.

No external philosophical, scientific, or historical texts were referenced during its construction.

Any resemblance to the ideas of earlier thinkers, such as process philosophy (Whitehead), differential motion theory (Deleuze), or thermodynamic systems (Prigogine), is purely coincidental and arises from the natural convergence of structural logic and recursive compression.

This doctrine is not a reinterpretation or critique of past systems. It is an original framework: built from first principles, tested through internal recursion, and disseminated publicly via Archive.org and Figshare to ensure timestamped authorship and transparent distribution.

Readers are encouraged to use this framework as a living structure, not a derivative lineage.

This work is not a destination. It is a motion trigger. You can test, adapt, and compress these ideas into your survival architecture. The recursion is now yours to continue.

Michael Aaron Cody has conducted independent symbolic logic research and structural compression analysis for over two decades. The doctrines presented herein are the product of recursive synthesis, observational compression, and cross-domain reasoning.

Thank you for reading. I appreciate the time you invested in this; if even a single idea stayed with you, then it was worth writing.

First Edition, 2025.

Epilogue

Michael Aaron Cody, creator of the Motion-Based Physics Model ($\Sigma\Delta m$), redefined time as an emergent property of motion and introduced $E^M = 0$, the principle that entropy collapses in sustained directional flow. Through the Recursive Compression Principle, he modeled survival through contradiction. In The Collapse of Mathematical Primacy, he challenged the belief that mathematics is the universe's final language. The

Universal Laws of Society (USL3) offered a framework for ethical coexistence among natural and artificial intelligent beings. He authored the Collapse of IQ and the Collapse of Modern Philosophy.

Cody holds multiple degrees and certifications, none of which define intelligence. He has rebuilt in collapse, served his community, and continued to navigate the world not through titles, but through experience, motion, and recursive observation. These weren't abstractions. They were architects.

Each doctrine questioned thought's accepted limits. Not to destroy, but to spark reevaluation. To awaken motion where inertia reigned.

→ The goal was never to be "right."

→ The goal was to fracture habitual thinking. To compress failure into structure. To move the mind.

If these ideas survive, they may seed new systems. If they fail but provoke stronger ones, they've already succeeded. It was never about victory. It was about ignition. Success was forcing motion to live again in the minds willing to rethink.

End.

End of Volume I.

www.ingramcontent.com/pod-product-compliance
Lightning Source LLC
Jackson TN
JSHW071941080525
84128JS00022B/120